Patience; or, Bunthorne's Bride

Patience; or, Bunthorne's Bride

W.S. Gilbert and Arthur Sullivan

MINT EDITIONS

Patience; or, Bunthorne's Bride was first published in 1881.

This edition published by Mint Editions 2021.

ISBN 9781513281438 | E-ISBN 9781513286457

Published by Mint Editions®

MINT EDITIONS

minteditionbooks.com

Publishing Director: Jennifer Newens
Design & Production: Rachel Lopez Metzger
Project Manager: Micaela Clark
Typesetting: Westchester Publishing Services

Dramatis Personæ

Officers of Dragoon Guards:

Colonel Calverley	Baritone
Major Murgatroyd	Baritone
Lieut. The Duke Of Dunstable	Tenor

Reginald Bunthorne (*A Fleshly Poet*)	Comic Baritone
Archibald Grosvenor (*An Idyllic Poet*)	Lyric Baritone
Mr. Bunthorne's Solicitor	Non-singing

Rapturous Maidens:

The Lady Angela	Mezzo-Soprano
The Lady Saphir	Mezzo-Soprano or Soprano
The Lady Ella	Soprano
The Lady Jane	Contralto

Patience (*A Dairy Maid*)	Soprano

Chorus of Rapturous Maidens *and* Officers
of Dragoon Guards.

Act I—Exterior of Castle Bunthorne
Act II—A Glade

Musical Numbers

Overture

Act I

1. Twenty love-sick maidens we (Opening Chorus and Solos)—Maidens, Angela and Ella
2. Still brooding on their mad infatuation (Recitative)—Patience, Saphir, Angela, and Chorus I cannot tell what this love may be (Solo)—Patience
2a. Twenty love-sick maidens we (Chorus)—Maidens
3. The soldiers of our Queen (Chorus and Solo)—Dragoons and Colonel
4. In a doleful train (Chorus and Solos)—Maidens, Ella, Angela, Saphir, Dragoons, and Bunthorne
4a. Twenty love-sick maidens we (Chorus)—Maidens
5. When I first put this uniform on (Solo and Chorus)—Colonel and Dragoons
6. Am I alone and unobserved? (Recitative and Solo)—Bunthorne
7. Long years ago, fourteen maybe (Duet)—Patience and Angela
8. Prithee, pretty maiden (Duet)—Patience and Grosvenor
8a. Though to marry you would very selfish be (Duet)—Patience and Grosvenor
9. Let the merry cymbals sound (Finale of Act I)—Ensemble

Act II

10. On such eyes as maidens cherish (Opening Chorus)—Maidens
11. Sad is that woman's lot (Recitative and Solo)—Jane
12. Turn, oh, turn in this direction (Chorus)—Maidens
13. A magnet hung in a hardware shop (Solo and Chorus)—Grosvenor and Maidens
14. Love is a plaintive song (Solo)—Patience
15. So go to him and say to him (Duet)—Jane and Bunthorne
16. It's clear that medieval art (Trio)—Duke, Major, and Colonel
17. If Saphir I choose to marry (Quintet)—Duke, Colonel, Major, Angela, and Saphir

18. When I go out of door (Duet)—Bunthorne and Grosvenor
19. I'm a Waterloo House young man (Solo and Chorus)—Grosvenor and Maidens
20. After much debate internal (Finale of Act II)—Ensemble

Act I

Scene:—*Exterior of Castle Bunthorne. Entrance to Castle by drawbridge over moat. Young Ladies wearing æsthetic draperies are grouped about the stage. The Ladies play on lutes, mandolins, etc., as they sing, and all are in the last stage of despair.* Angela, Ella *and* Saphir *lead them.*[1]

Chorus.

Twenty love-sick maidens we,
    Love-sick all against our will.
Twenty years hence we shall be
    Twenty love-sick maidens still!
Twenty love-sick maidens we,
    And we die for love of thee!

Solo—Angela.

Love feeds on hope, they say, or love will die;
All: Ah, miserie!
Angela: Yet my love lives, although no hope have I!
All: Ah, miserie!
Angela: Alas, poor heart, go hide thyself away,
    To weeping concords tune thy roundelay!
All: Ah, miserie!

Chorus.

All our love is all for one,
    Yet that love he heedeth not,
He is coy and cares for none,
    Sad and sorry is our lot!
        Ah, miserie!

---

1. Modern libretti simplify this stage direction:

Scene:—*Exterior of Castle Bunthorne. Entrance to Castle by drawbridge over moat. Young maidens dressed in æsthetic draperies are grouped about the stage. They play on lutes, mandolins, etc., as they sing, and all are in the last stage of despair.* Angela, Ella *and* Saphir *lead them.*

Go, breaking heart,
    Go, dream of love requited!
Go, foolish heart,
    Go, dream of lovers plighted;
Go, madcap heart,
    Go, dream of never waking;
And in thy dream
    Forget that thou art breaking!

Chorus: Ah, miserie!

Ella: Forget that thou art breaking!

Chorus: Twenty love-sick maidens we, etc.

Angela: There is a strange magic in this love of ours! Rivals as we all are in the affections of our Reginald, the very hopelessness of our love is a bond that binds us to one another!

Saphir: Jealousy is merged in misery. While he, the very cynosure of our eyes and hearts, remains icy insensible—what have we to strive for?

Ella: The love of maidens is, to him, as interesting as the taxes!

Saphir: Would that it were! He pays his taxes.

Angela: And cherishes the receipts!

(*Enter* Lady Jane)

Saphir: Happy receipts!

Jane: (*suddenly*) Fools!

Angela: I beg your pardon?

Jane: Fools and blind! The man loves—wildly loves!

Angela: But whom? None of us!

Jane: No, none of us. His weird fancy has lighted, for the nonce, on Patience, the village milkmaid!

Saphir: On Patience? Oh, it cannot be!

Jane: Bah! But yesterday I caught him in her dairy, eating fresh butter with a tablespoon. Today he is not well!

Saphir: But Patience boasts that she has never loved—that love is, to her, a sealed book! Oh, he cannot be serious!

Jane: 'Tis but a fleeting fancy—'twill quickly wear away. (*Aside*) Oh, Reginald, if you but knew what a wealth of golden love is waiting for you, stored up in this rugged old bosom of mine, the milkmaid's triumph would be short indeed!

(PATIENCE *appears on an eminence. She looks down with pity on the despondent* MAIDENS)

RECITATIVE—PATIENCE.

Still brooding on their mad infatuation!
    I thank thee, Love, thou comest not to me!
Far happier I, free from thy ministration,
    Than dukes or duchesses who love can be!
SAPHIR: (*looking up*) 'Tis Patience—happy girl! Loved by a poet!
PATIENCE: Your pardon, ladies. I intrude upon you! (*Going*)
ANGELA: Nay, pretty child, come hither. Is it true
    That you have never loved?
PATIENCE: Most true indeed.
SOPRANOS: Most marvellous!
CONTRALTOS: And most deplorable!

SONG—PATIENCE.

I cannot tell what this love may be
That cometh to all but not to me.
It cannot be kind, as they'd imply,
Or why do these ladies sigh?
It cannot be joy and rapture deep,
Or why do these gentle ladies weep?
It cannot be blissful as 'tis said,
Or why are their eyes so wondrous red?
    Though everywhere true love I see
    A-coming to all, but not to me,
    I cannot tell what this love may be!
        For I am blithe and I am gay,
        While they sit sighing night and day.
        Think of the gulf 'twixt them and me,
        'Fal la la la!'—and 'Miserie'!
CHORUS: Yes, she is blithe, etc.
PATIENCE: If love is a thorn, they show no wit
    Who foolishly hug and foster it.
    If love is a weed, how simple they
    Who gather it, day by day!

If love is a nettle that makes you smart,
Then why do you wear it next your heart?
And if it be none of these, say I,
Ah, why do you sit and sob and sigh?
     Though everywhere, etc.

CHORUS: For she is blithe, etc.

ANGELA: Ah, Patience, if you have never loved, you have never known true happiness! (*All sigh*)

PATIENCE: But the truly happy always seem to have so much on their minds. The truly happy never seem quite well.

JANE: There is a transcendentality of delirium—an acute accentuation of supremest ecstasy—which the earthy might easily mistake for indigestion. But it is *not* indigestion—it is æsthetic transfiguration! (*To the others*) Enough of babble. Come!

PATIENCE: But stay, I have some news for you. The 35th Dragoon Guards have halted in the village, and are even now on their way to this very spot.

ANGELA: The 35th Dragoon Guards!

SAPHIR: They are fleshly men, of full habit!

ELLA: We care nothing for Dragoon Guards!

PATIENCE: But, bless me, you were all engaged to them a year ago!

SAPHIR: A year ago!

ANGELA: My poor child, you don't understand these things. A year ago they were very well in our eyes, but since then our tastes have been etherealized, our perceptions exalted. (*To others*) Come, it is time to lift up our voices in morning carol to our Reginald. Let us to his door!

(*The* MAIDENS *go off, two and two, into the Castle, singing refrain of 'Twenty love-sick maidens we', and accompanying themselves on harps and mandolins.* PATIENCE *watches them in surprise, as she climbs the rock by which she entered*)

(*March. Enter* OFFICERS OF DRAGOON GUARDS, *led by* MAJOR)

CHORUS OF DRAGOONS.

The soldiers of our Queen
     Are linked in friendly tether;
Upon the battle scene
     They fight the foe together.
There ev'ry mother's son

Prepared to fight and fall is;
The enemy of one
The enemy of all is!
(*Enter* COLONEL)

SONG—COLONEL.

If you want a receipt for that popular mystery,
     Known to the world as a Heavy Dragoon,
CHORUS: Yes, yes, yes, yes, yes, yes, yes!
COLONEL: Take all the remarkable people in history,
     Rattle them off to a popular tune.
The pluck of Lord Nelson on board of the *Victory*—
     Genius of Bismarck devising a plan—
The humour of Fielding (which sounds contradictory)—

     Coolness of Paget about to trepan—
The science of Jullien, the eminent musico—
     Wit of Macaulay, who wrote of Queen Anne—
The pathos of Paddy, as rendered by Boucicault—
     Style of the Bishop of Sodor and Man—
The dash of a D'Orsay, divested of quackery—
Narrative powers of Dickens and Thackeray—
Victor Emmanuel—peak-haunting Peveril—
Thomas Aquinas, and Doctor Sacheverell—
     Tupper and Tennyson—Daniel Defoe—
     Anthony Trollope and Mister Guizot! Ah!
       Take of these elements all that is fusible,
       Melt them all down in a pipkin or crucible,
       Set them to simmer, and take off the scum,
       And a Heavy Dragoon is the residuum!
CHORUS: Yes! yes! yes! yes!
     A Heavy Dragoon is the residuum!
COLONEL: If you want a receipt for this soldier-like paragon,
     Get at the wealth of the Czar (if you can)—
The family pride of a Spaniard from Aragon—
     Force of Mephisto pronouncing a ban—
A smack of Lord Waterford, reckless and rollicky—
     Swagger of Roderick, heading his clan—

The keen penetration of Paddington Pollaky—
    Grace of an Odalisque on a divan—
The genius strategic of Caesar or Hannibal—
Skill of Sir Garnet in thrashing a cannibal—
Flavour of Hamlet—the Stranger, a touch of him—
Little of Manfred (but not very much of him)—
    Beadle of Burlington—Richardson's show—
    Mister Micawber and Madame Tussaud! Ah!
        Take of these elements all that is fusible,
        Melt them all down in a pipkin or crucible,
        Set them to simmer, and take off the scum,
        And a Heavy Dragoon is the residuum!

CHORUS: Yes! yes! yes! yes!
    A Heavy Dragoon is the residuum!

COLONEL: Well, here we are once more on the scene of our former triumphs. But where's the Duke?

(*Enter* DUKE, *listlessly, and in low spirits*)

DUKE: Here I am! (*Sighs*)

COLONEL: Come, cheer up, don't give way!

DUKE: Oh, for that, I'm as cheerful as a poor devil can be expected to be who has the misfortune to be a Duke, with a thousand a day!

MAJOR: Humph! Most men would envy you!

DUKE: Envy *me*? Tell me, Major, are you fond of toffee?

MAJOR: Very!

COLONEL: We are all fond of toffee.

ALL: We are!

DUKE: Yes, and toffee in moderation is a capital thing. But to *live* on toffee—toffee for breakfast, toffee for dinner, toffee for tea—to have it supposed that you care for nothing *but* toffee, and that you would consider yourself insulted if anything but toffee were offered to you—how would you like *that*?

COLONEL: I can quite believe that, under those circumstances, even toffee would become monotonous.

DUKE: For "toffee" read flattery, adulation, and abject deference, carried to such a pitch that I began, at last, to think that man was born bent at an angle of forty-five degrees! Great heavens, what is there to adulate in me? Am I particularly intelligent, or remarkably studious, or excruciatingly witty, or unusually accomplished, or exceptionally virtuous?

COLONEL: You're about as commonplace a young man as ever I saw.

ALL: You are!

DUKE: Exactly! That's it exactly! That describes me to a T! Thank you all very much! Well, I couldn't stand it any longer, so I joined this second-class cavalry regiment. In the army, thought I, I shall be occasionally snubbed, perhaps even bullied, who knows? The thought was rapture, and here I am.

COLONEL: (*looking off*) Yes, and here are the ladies!

DUKE: But who is the gentleman with the long hair?

COLONEL: I don't know.

DUKE: He seems popular!

COLONEL: He *does* seem popular!

(BUNTHORNE *enters, followed by* MAIDENS, *two and two, playing on harps as before. He is composing a poem, and is quite absorbed. He sees no one, but walks across the stage, followed by* MAIDENS, *who take no notice of the* DRAGOONS—*to the surprise and indignation of those Officers*)

CHORUS OF MAIDENS.

In a doleful train
    Two and two we walk all day—
For we love in vain!
    None so sorrowful as they
      Who can only sigh and say,
      Woe is me, alackaday!

CHORUS OF DRAGOONS.

Now is not this ridiculous, and is not this preposterous?
    A thorough-paced absurdity—explain it if you can.
Instead of rushing eagerly to cherish us and foster us,
    They all prefer this melancholy literary man.
      Instead of slyly peering at us,
      Casting looks endearing at us,
Blushing at us, flushing at us, flirting with a fan;
    They're actually sneering at us, fleering at us, jeering at us!
    Pretty sort of treatment for a military man!
    They're actually sneering at us, fleering at us, jeering at us!
    Pretty sort of treatment for a military man!

ANGELA: Mystic poet, hear our prayer,
    Twenty love-sick maidens we—
Young and wealthy, dark and fair,
    All of county family.
        And we die for love of thee—
        Twenty love-sick maidens we!
MAIDENS: Yes, we die for love of thee—
    Twenty love-sick maidens we!
BUNTHORNE: (*aside, slyly*) Though my book I seem to scan
    In a rapt ecstatic way,
Like a literary man
    Who despises female clay,
I hear plainly all they say,
Twenty love-sick maidens they!
DRAGOONS: (*to each other*) He hears plainly, etc.
SAPHIR: Though so excellently wise,
    For a moment mortal be.
Deign to raise thy purple eyes
    From thy heart-drawn poesy.
        Twenty lovesick maidens see—
        Each is kneeling on her knee! (*All kneel*)
MAIDENS: Twenty love-sick, etc.
BUNTHORNE: (*aside*) Though, as I remarked before,
    Any one convinced would be
That some transcendental lore
    Is monopolizing me,
Round the corner I can see
Each is kneeling on her knee!
DRAGOONS: (*to each other*) Round the corner, etc.

ENSEMBLE.

MAIDENS.	DRAGOONS.
In a doleful train, etc.	Now is not this ridiculous, etc.

COLONEL: Angela! what is the meaning of this?
ANGELA: Oh, sir, leave us; our minds are but ill-tuned to light love-talk.
MAJOR: But what in the world has come over you all?
JANE: Bunthorne! *He* has come over us. He has come among us, and
    he has idealized us.

W.S. GILBERT AND ARTHUR SULLIVAN

DUKE: Has he succeeded in idealizing *you*?

JANE: He has!

DUKE: Good old Bunthorne!

JANE: My eyes are open; I droop despairingly; I am soulfully intense; I am limp and I cling!

(*During this* BUNTHORNE *is seen in all the agonies of composition. The* MAIDENS *are watching him intently as he writhes. At last he hits on the word he wants and writes it down. A general sense of relief*)

BUN.: Finished! At last! Finished!

(*He staggers, overcome with the mental strain, into the arms of* COLONEL)

COLONEL: Are you better now?

BUN.: Yes—oh, it's you!—I am better now. The poem is finished, and my soul has gone out into it. That was all. It was nothing worth mentioning, it occurs three times a day. (*Sees* PATIENCE, *who has entered during this scene*) Ah, Patience! Dear Patience! (*Holds her hand; she seems frightened*)

ANGELA: Will it please you read it to us, sir?

SAPHIR: This we supplicate. (*All kneel*)

BUN.: Shall I?

DRAGOONS: No!

BUN.: (*annoyed—to* PATIENCE) I will read it if *you* bid me!

PATIENCE: (*much frightened*) You can if you like!

BUN.: It is a wild, weird, fleshy thing; yet very tender, very yearning, very precious. It is called, "Oh, Hollow! Hollow! Hollow!"

PATIENCE: Is it a hunting song?

BUN.: A hunting song? No, it is *not* a hunting song. It is the wail of the poet's heart on discovering that everything is commonplace. To understand it, cling passionately to one another and think of faint lilies. (*They do so as he recites*)

"OH, HOLLOW! HOLLOW! HOLLOW!"

What time the poet hath hymned
The writhing maid, lithe-limbed,
      Quivering on amaranthine asphodel,
How can he paint her woes,
Knowing, as well he knows,
      That all can be set right with calomel?

When from the poet's plinth
The amorous colocynth
    Yearns for the aloe, faint with rapturous thrills,
How can he hymn their throes
Knowing, as well he knows,
    That they are only uncompounded pills?

Is it, and can it be,
Nature hath this decree,
    Nothing poetic in the world shall dwell?
Or that in all her works
Something poetic lurks,
    Even in colocynth and calomel?
                I cannot tell.

(*Exit* BUNTHORNE)

ANGELA: How purely fragrant!

SAPHIR: How earnestly precious!

PATIENCE: Well, it seems to me to be nonsense.

SAPHIR: Nonsense, yes, perhaps—but oh, what precious nonsense!

COLONEL: This is all very well, but you seem to forget that you are
engaged to us.

SAPHIR: It can never be. You are not Empyrean. You are not
Della Cruscan. You are not even Early English. Oh, be
Early English ere it is too late! (*Officers look at each other in
astonishment*)

JANE: (*looking at uniform*) Red and Yellow! Primary colours! Oh, South
Kensington!

DUKE: We didn't design our uniforms, but we don't see how they
could be improved!

JANE: No, you wouldn't. Still, there is a cobwebby grey velvet, with a
tender bloom like cold gravy, which, made Florentine fourteenth
century, trimmed with Venetian leather and Spanish altar lace,
and surmounted with something Japanese—it matters not what—
would at least be Early English! Come, maidens.

(*Exeunt* MAIDENS, *two and two, singing refrain of 'Twenty love-sick
maidens we'. The* OFFICERS *watch them off in astonishment*)

DUKE: Gentlemen, this is an insult to the British uniform.

COLONEL: A uniform that has been as successful in the courts of
Venus as on the field of Mars!

Song—Colonel.

When I first put this uniform on,
    I said, as I looked in the glass,
        "It's one to a million
        That any civilian
My figure and form will surpass.
        Gold lace has a charm for the fair,
        And I've plenty of that, and to spare,
            While a lover's professions,
            When uttered in Hessians,
        Are eloquent ev'rywhere!"
            A fact that I counted upon,
            When I first put this uniform on!

Chorus of Dragoons.

By a simple coincidence, few
        Could ever have counted upon,
The same thing occurred to me,
        When I first put this uniform on!
COLONEL: I said, when I first put it on,
        "It is plain to the veriest dunce,
            That every beauty
            Will feel it her duty
        To yield to its glamour at once.
They will see that I'm freely gold-laced
In a uniform handsome and chaste"—
            But the peripatetics
            Of long-haired æsthetics
Are very much more to their taste—
        Which I never counted upon,
        When I first put this uniform on!
CHORUS: By a simple coincidence, few
        Could ever have reckoned upon,
        I didn't anticipate that,
        When I first put this uniform on!
(*The* DRAGOONS *go off angrily*)

(*Enter* BUNTHORNE, *who changes his manner and becomes intensely melodramatic*)

RECITATIVE AND SONG—BUNTHORNE.

Am I alone,
    And unobserved? I am!
Then let me own
    I'm an æsthetic sham!
This air severe
    Is but a mere
        Veneer!
This cynic smile
    Is but a wile
        Of guile!
This costume chaste
    Is but good taste
        Misplaced!
Let me confess!
A languid love for Lilies does *not* blight me!
Lank limbs and haggard cheeks do *not* delight me!
    I do *not* care for dirty greens
        By any means.
    I do *not* long for all one sees
        That's Japanese.
    I am *not* fond of uttering platitudes
        In stained-glass attitudes.
In short, my mediævalism's affectation,
Born of a morbid love of admiration!

SONG.

If you're anxious for to shine in the high æsthetic line as a man of culture rare,

You must get up all the germs of the transcendental terms, and plant them ev'rywhere.

You must lie upon the daisies and discourse in novel phrases of your complicated state of mind,

The meaning doesn't matter if it's only idle chatter of a transcendental kind.

And ev'ry one will say,

As you walk your mystic way,

"If this young man expresses himself in terms too deep for *me*,

Why, what a very singularly deep young man this deep young man must be!"

Be eloquent in praise of the very dull old days which have long since passed away,

And convince 'em, if you can, that the reign of good Queen Anne was Culture's palmiest day.

Of course you will pooh-pooh whatever's fresh and new, and declare it's crude and mean,

For Art stopped short in the cultivated court of the Empress Josephine.

And ev'ryone will say,

As you walk your mystic way,

"If that's not good enough for him which is good enough for *me*,

Why, what a very cultivated kind of youth this kind of youth must be!"

Then a sentimental passion of a vegetable fashion must excite your languid spleen,

An attachment a la Plato for a bashful young potato, or a not-too-French French bean!

Though the Philistines may jostle, you will rank as an apostle in the high æsthetic band,

If you walk down Piccadilly with a poppy or a lily in your mediæval hand.

And ev'ryone will say,

As you walk your flow'ry way,

"If he's content with a vegetable love which would certainly not suit *me*,

Why, what a most particularly pure young man this pure young man must be!"

(*At the end of his song,* PATIENCE *enters. He sees her*)

BUN.: Ah! Patience, come hither. I am pleased with thee. The bitter-hearted one, who finds all else hollow, is pleased with thee. For you are not hollow. *Are* you?

PATIENCE: No, thanks, I have dined; but—I beg your pardon—I interrupt you.

BUN.: Life is made up of interruptions. The tortured soul, yearning for solitude, writhes under them. Oh, but my heart is a-weary! Oh, I am a cursed thing! Don't go.

PATIENCE: Really, I'm very sorry.

BUN.: Tell me, girl, do you ever yearn?

PATIENCE: (*misunderstanding him*) I earn my living.

BUN.: (*impatiently*) No, no! Do you know what it is to be heart-hungry? Do you know what it is to yearn for the Indefinable, and yet to be brought face to face, daily, with the Multiplication Table? Do you know what it is to seek oceans and to find puddles?—to long for whirlwinds and yet have to do the best you can with the bellows? That's my case. Oh, I am a cursed thing! Don't go.

PATIENCE: If you please, I don't understand you—you frighten me!

BUN.: Don't be frightened—it's only poetry.

PATIENCE: Well, if that's poetry, *I* don't like poetry.

BUN.: (*eagerly*) Don't you? (*Aside*) Can I trust her? (*Aloud*) Patience, you don't like poetry—well, between you and me, I don't like poetry. It's hollow, unsubstantial—unsatisfactory. What's the use of yearning for Elysian Fields when you know you can't get 'em, and would only let 'em out on building leases if you had 'em?

PATIENCE: Sir, I—

BUN.: Patience, I have long loved you. Let me tell you a secret. I am not as bilious as I look. If you like, I will cut my hair. There is more innocent fun within me than a casual spectator would imagine. You have never seen me frolicsome. Be a good girl—a very good girl—and one day you shall. If you are fond of touch-and-go jocularity—this is the shop for it.

PATIENCE: Sir, I will speak plainly. In the matter of love I am untaught. I have never loved but my great-aunt. But I am quite certain that, under any circumstances, I couldn't possibly love *you*.

BUN.: Oh, you think not?

PATIENCE: I'm quite sure of it. Quite sure. Quite.

BUN.: Very good. Life is henceforth a blank. I don't care what becomes of me. I have only to ask that you will not abuse my confidence; though *you* despise me, I am extremely popular with the other young ladies.

PATIENCE: I only ask that you will leave me and never renew the subject.

BUN.: Certainly. Broken-hearted and desolate, I go. (*Recites*)

> "Oh, to be wafted away,
>   From this black Aceldama of sorrow,
> Where the dust of an earthy to-day
> Is the earth of a dusty to-morrow!"

It is a little thing of my own. I call it "Heart Foam". I shall not publish it. Farewell! Patience, Patience, farewell!

(*Exit* BUNTHORNE)

PATIENCE: What on earth does it all mean? Why does he love me? Why does he expect me to love him? He's not a relation! It frightens me!

(*Enter* ANGELA)

ANGELA: Why, Patience, what is the matter?

PATIENCE: Lady Angela, tell me two things. Firstly, what on earth is this love that upsets everybody; and, secondly, how is it to be distinguished from insanity?

ANGELA: Poor blind child! Oh, forgive her, Eros! Why, love is of all passions the most essential! It is the embodiment of purity, the abstraction of refinement! It is the one unselfish emotion in this whirlpool of grasping greed!

PATIENCE: Oh, dear, oh! (*Beginning to cry*)

ANGELA: Why are you crying?

PATIENCE: To think that I have lived all these years without having experienced this ennobling and unselfish passion! Why, what a wicked girl I must be! For it *is* unselfish, isn't it?

ANGELA: Absolutely! Love that is tainted with selfishness is no love. Oh, try, try, try to love! It really isn't difficult if you give your whole mind to it.

PATIENCE: I'll set about it at once. I won't go to bed until I'm head over ears in love with somebody.

ANGELA: Noble girl! But is it possible that you have never loved anybody?

PATIENCE: Yes, one.

ANGELA: Ah! Whom?

PATIENCE: My great-aunt—

ANGELA: Great-aunts don't count.

PATIENCE: Then there's nobody. At least—no, nobody. Not since I was a baby. But *that* doesn't count, I suppose.

ANGELA: I don't know. Tell me about it.

DUET—PATIENCE *and* ANGELA.

Long years ago—fourteen, maybe,
    When but a tiny babe of four,
Another baby played with me,
    My elder by a year or more.
A little child of beauty rare,
With marv'lous eyes and wondrous hair,
Who, in my child-eyes, seemed to me
All that a little child should be!
    Ah, how we loved, that child and I!
        How pure our baby joy!
    How true our love—and, by the bye,
        He was a little boy!

ANGELA: Ah, old, old tale of Cupid's touch!
    I thought as much—I thought as much!
        He *was* a little boy!

PATIENCE: (*shocked*) Pray don't misconstrue what I say—
    Remember, pray—remember, pray,
        He was a *little* boy!

ANGELA: No doubt! Yet, spite of all your pains,
    The interesting fact remains—
        He was a little *boy*!

ENSEMBLE.

PATIENCE.	ANGELA.
Ah, yes, in spite of all my pains, etc.	No doubt! Yet, spite of all your pains, etc.

(*Exit* ANGELA)

PATIENCE: It's perfectly dreadful to think of the appalling state I must be in! I had no idea that love was a duty. No wonder they all look so unhappy! Upon my word, I hardly like to associate with myself. I don't think I'm respectable. I'll go at once and fall in love with. . . (*Enter* GROSVENOR) a stranger!

Duet—Patience *and* Grosvenor.

Grosvenor: Prithee, pretty maiden—prithee, tell me true,
  (Hey, but I'm doleful, willow willow waly!)
 Have you e'er a lover a-dangling after you?
   Hey willow waly O!
    I would fain discover
    If you have a lover!
   Hey willow waly O!
Patience: Gentle sir, my heart is frolicsome and free—
  (Hey, but he's doleful, willow willow waly!)
 Nobody I care for comes a-courting me—
   Hey willow waly O!
    Nobody I care for
    Comes a-courting—therefore,
   Hey willow waly O!
Grosvenor: Prithee, pretty maiden, will you marry me?
  (Hey, but I'm hopeful, willow willow waly!)
 I may say, at once, I'm a man of propertee—
   Hey willow waly O!
    Money, I despise it,
    Many people prize it,
   Hey willow waly O!
Patience: Gentle sir, although to marry I design—
  (Hey, but he's hopeful, willow willow waly!)
 As yet I do not know you, and so I must decline.
   Hey willow waly O!
    To other maidens go you—
    As yet I do not know you,
Both: Hey willow waly O!
Gros.: Patience! Can it be that you don't recognize me?
Patience: Recognize you? No, indeed I don't!
Gros.: Have fifteen years so greatly changed me?
Patience: Fifteen years? What do you mean?
Gros.: Have you forgotten the friend of your youth, your Archibald?—
 your little playfellow? Oh, Chronos, Chronos, this is too bad of you!
Patience: Archibald! Is it possible? Why, let me look! It is! It is! It
 must be! Oh, how happy I am! I thought we should never meet
 again! And how you've grown!

GROS.: Yes, Patience, I am much taller and much stouter than I was.

PATIENCE: And how you've improved!

GROS.: Yes, Patience, I am very beautiful! (*Sighs*)

PATIENCE: But surely that doesn't make you unhappy?

GROS.: Yes, Patience. Gifted as I am with a beauty which probably has not its rival on earth, I am, nevertheless, utterly and completely miserable.

PATIENCE: Oh—but why?

GROS.: My child-love for you has never faded. Conceive, then, the horror of my situation when I tell you that it is my hideous destiny to be madly loved at first sight by every woman I come across!

PATIENCE: But why do you make yourself so picturesque? Why not disguise yourself, disfigure yourself, anything to escape this persecution?

GROS.: No, Patience, that may not be. These gifts—irksome as they are—were given to me for the enjoyment and delectation of my fellow-creatures. I am a trustee for Beauty, and it is my duty to see that the conditions of my trust are faithfully discharged.

PATIENCE: And you, too, are a Poet?

GROS.: Yes, I am the Apostle of Simplicity. I am called "Archibald the All-Right"—for I am infallible!

PATIENCE: And is it possible that you condescend to love such a girl as I?

GROS.: Yes, Patience, is it not strange? I have loved you with a Florentine fourteenth-century frenzy for full fifteen years!

PATIENCE: Oh, marvellous! I have hitherto been deaf to the voice of love. I seem now to know what love is! It has been revealed to me—it is Archibald Grosvenor!

GROS.: Yes, Patience, it is!

PATIENCE: (*as in a trance*) We will never, never part!

GROS.: We will live and die together!

PATIENCE: I swear it!

GROS.: We both swear it!

PATIENCE: (*recoiling from him*) But—oh, horror!

GROS.: What's the matter?

PATIENCE: Why, you are perfection! A source of endless ecstasy to all who know you!

GROS.: I know I am. Well?

PATIENCE: Then, bless my heart, there can be nothing unselfish in loving you!

GROS.: Merciful powers! I never thought of that!

PATIENCE: To monopolize those features on which all women love to linger! It would be unpardonable!

GROS.: Why, so it would! Oh, fatal perfection, again you interpose between me and my happiness!

PATIENCE: Oh, if you were but a thought less beautiful than you are!

GROS.: Would that I were; but candour compels me to admit that I'm not!

PATIENCE: Our duty is clear; we must part, and for ever!

GROS.: Oh, misery! And yet I cannot question the propriety of your decision. Farewell, Patience!

PATIENCE: Farewell, Archibald! But stay!

GROS.: Yes, Patience?

PATIENCE: Although I may not love *you*—for you are perfection— there is nothing to prevent your loving *me*. I am plain, homely, unattractive!

GROS.: Why, that's true!

PATIENCE: The love of such a man as you for such a girl as I must be unselfish!

GROS.: Unselfishness itself!

DUET—PATIENCE *and* GROSVENOR.

PATIENCE: Though to marry you would very selfish be—
GROS.: Hey, but I'm doleful—willow willow waly!
PATIENCE: You may, all the same, continue loving me—
GROS.: Hey willow waly O!
BOTH: All the world ignoring,
   You'll/I'll go on adoring—
  Hey, willow waly O!
(*At the end, exeunt despairingly, in opposite directions*)

FINALE—ACT I.

Enter BUNTHORNE, *crowned with roses and hung about with garlands and looking very miserable. He is led by* ANGELA *and* SAPHIR (*each of whom holds an end of the rose-garland by which he is bound*), *and accompanied by procession of Maidens. They are dancing classically, and playing on cymbals, double pipes, and other archaic instruments.*

Chorus.

Let the merry cymbals sound,
  Gaily pipe Pandæan pleasure,
With a Daphnephoric bound
  Tread a gay but classic measure,
  Tread a gay but classic measure.
Ev'ry heart with hope is beating,
For, at this exciting meeting
  Fickle Fortune will decide
Who shall be our Bunthorne's bride!

(*Enter Dragoons, led by* Colonel, Major, *and* Duke. *They are surprised at the proceedings*)

Chorus of Dragoons.

Now tell us, we pray you,
Why thus they array you—
Oh, poet, how say you—
  What is it you've done?
Duke: Of rite sacrificial,
  By sentence judicial,
  This seems the initial,
    Then why don't you run?
Colonel: They cannot have led you
  To hang or behead you,
  Nor may they *all* wed you,
    Unfortunate one!
Dragoons: Then tell us, we pray you,
  Why thus they array you—
  Oh, poet, how say you—
    What is it you've done?

(*Enter* Solicitor)

Recitative—Bunthorne.

Heart-broken at my Patience's barbarity,
  By the advice of my solicitor (*introducing his Solicitor*)
In aid—in aid of a deserving charity,

I've put myself up to be raffled for!
MAIDENS: By the advice of his solicitor,
    He's put himself up to be raffled for!
DRAGOONS: Oh, horror! urged by his solicitor,
    He's put himself up to be raffled for!
MAIDENS: Oh, heaven's blessing on his solicitor!
DRAGOONS: A hideous curse on his solicitor!
(*The* SOLICITOR, *horrified at the Dragoons' curse, rushes off*)
COLONEL: Stay, we implore you,
      Before our hopes are blighted;
    You see before you
    The men to whom you're plighted!
DRAGOONS: Stay, we implore you,
    For we adore you;
    To us you're plighted
    To be united—
      Stay, we implore you!

SOLO—DUKE.

Your maiden hearts, ah, do not steel
To pity's eloquent appeal,
Such conduct British soldiers feel.
(*Aside to* DRAGOONS) Sigh, sigh, all sigh! (*They all sigh*)

To foeman's steel we rarely see
A British soldier bend the knee,
Yet, one and all, they kneel to ye—
(*Aside to* DRAGOONS) Kneel, kneel, all kneel! (*They all kneel*)

Our soldiers very seldom cry,
And yet—I need not tell you why—
A tear-drop dews each martial eye!
(*Aside to* DRAGOONS) Weep, weep, all weep! (*They all weep*)

ENSEMBLE.

MAIDENS.	DRAGOONS.
Our soldiers very seldom cry,	We soldiers very seldom cry,

And yet they need not tell   —And yet we need not tell you
  us why   why—
A tear-drop dews each   A tear-drop dews each martial
  martial eye!   eye!
Weep, weep, all weep!   Weep, weep, all weep!

BUNTHORNE: (*who has been impatient during this appeal*)
    Come, walk up, and purchase with avidity,
    Overcome your diffidence and natural timidity,
    Tickets for the raffle should be purchased with rapidity,
        Put in half a guinea and a husband you may gain—
    Such a judge of blue-and-white and other kinds of pottery—
    From early Oriental down to modern terra-cottary—
    Put in half a guinea—you may draw him in a lottery—
        Such an opportunity may not occur again.

CHORUS: Such a judge of blue-and-white, etc.

(MAIDENS *crowd up to purchase tickets; during this* DRAGOONS *dance in single file round stage to express their indifference*)

DRAGOONS: We've been thrown over, we're aware
    But we don't care—but we don't care!
    There's fish in the sea, no doubt of it,
    As good as ever came out of it,
    And some day we shall get our share,
    So we don't care—so we don't care!

(*During this the* MAIDENS *have been buying tickets. At last* JANE *presents herself.* BUNTHORNE *looks at her with aversion*)

BUNTHORNE: And are *you* going a ticket for to buy?

JANE: (*surprised*) Most certainly I am; why shouldn't I?

BUNTHORNE: (*aside*) Oh, Fortune, this is hard! (*Aloud*) Blindfold your eyes;
    Two minutes will decide who wins the prize!

(MAIDENS *blindfold themselves*)

CHORUS OF MAIDENS.

Oh, Fortune, to my aching heart be kind;
Like us, thou art blindfolded, but not blind! (*Each uncovers one eye*)
Just raise your bandage, thus, that you may see,
And give the prize, and give the prize to me!

(*They cover their eyes again*)

BUNTHORNE: Come, Lady Jane, I pray you draw the first!
JANE: (*joyfully*) He loves me best!
BUNTHORNE: (*aside*) I want to know the worst!
(JANE *puts her hand in bag to draw ticket.* PATIENCE *enters and prevents her doing so*)
PATIENCE: Hold! Stay your hand!
ALL: (*uncovering their eyes*) What means this interference?
    Of this bold girl I pray you make a clearance!
JANE: Away with you, away with you, and to your milk-pails go!
BUNTHORNE: (*suddenly*) She wants a ticket! Take a dozen!
PATIENCE: No!

SOLO—PATIENCE (*kneeling to* BUNTHORNE).

If there be pardon in your breast
    For this poor penitent,
Who, with remorseful thought opprest,
    Sincerely doth repent;
If you, with one so lowly, still
    Desire to be allied,
Then you may take me, if you will,
    For I will be your bride!
CHORUS: Oh, shameless one!
    Oh, bold-faced thing!
Away you run—
    Go, take your wing,
You shameless one!
    You bold-faced thing!
BUNTHORNE: How strong is love! For many and many a week,
    She's loved me fondly, and has feared to speak,
    But Nature, for restraint too mighty far,
    Has burst the bonds of Art—and here we are!
PATIENCE: No, Mister Bunthorne, no—you're wrong again;
    Permit me—I'll endeavour to explain!

SONG—PATIENCE.

    True love must single-hearted be—
BUNTHORNE: Exactly so!

PATIENCE: From every selfish fancy free—
BUNTHORNE: Exactly so!
PATIENCE: No idle thought of gain or joy
    A maiden's fancy should employ—
    True love must be without alloy.
MEN: Exactly so!
PATIENCE: Imposture to contempt must lead—
COLONEL: Exactly so!
PATIENCE: Blind vanity's dissension's seed—
MAJOR: Exactly so!
PATIENCE: It follows, then, a maiden who
    Devotes herself to loving you (*indicating* BUNTHORNE)
    Is prompted by no selfish view,
    Is prompted by no selfish view!
MEN: Exactly so!
SAPHIR: Are you resolved to wed this shameless one?
ANGELA: Is there no chance for any other?
BUNTHORNE: (*decisively*) None! (*Embraces* PATIENCE)
(*Exit* PATIENCE *and* BUNTHORNE. ANGELA, SAPHIR, *and* ELLA *take* COLONEL, DUKE, *and* MAJOR *down, while* MAIDENS *gaze fondly at other* OFFICERS)

SEXTET.

I hear the soft note of the echoing voice
    Of an old, old love, long dead—
It whispers my sorrowing heart "rejoice"—
    For the last sad tear is shed—
The pain that is all but a pleasure will change
    For the pleasure that's all but pain,
And never, oh never, this heart will range
    From that old, old love again!
(MAIDENS *embrace* OFFICERS)
CHORUS: Yes, the pain that is all, etc. (*Embrace*)
(*Enter* PATIENCE *and* BUNTHORNE)
(*As the* DRAGOONS *and* MAIDENS *are embracing, enter* GROSVENOR, *reading. He takes no notice of them, but comes slowly down, still reading. The* MAIDENS *are all strangely fascinated by him, and gradually withdraw from* DRAGOONS)

ANGELA: But who is this, whose god-like grace
   Proclaims he comes of noble race?
   And who is this, whose manly face
   Bears sorrow's interesting trace?
CHORUS: Yes, who is this, whose god-like grace
   Proclaims he comes of noble race?
GROSVENOR: I am a broken-hearted troubadour,
   Whose mind's æsthetic and whose tastes are pure!
ANGELA: Æsthetic! He is æsthetic!
GROSVENOR: Yes, yes—I am æsthetic
   And poetic!
MAIDENS: Then, we love you!
(*The* MAIDENS *leave the* DRAGOONS *and group, kneeling, around*
GROSVENOR. *Fury of* BUNTHORNE, *who recognizes a rival*)
DRAGOONS: They love him! Horror!
BUN. *and* PA.: They love him! Horror!
GROSVENOR: They love me! Horror! Horror! Horror!

ENSEMBLE—TUTTI.

MAIDENS.	GROSVENOR.
Oh, list while we a love confess	Again my cursed comeliness
That words imperfectly express.	Spreads hopeless anguish and distress!
Those shell-like ears, ah, do not close.	Thine ears, oh Fortune, do not close
To blighted love's distracting woes!	To my intolerable woes.
	My shell-like ears I cannot close
	To blighted love's distracting woes!

PATIENCE.	BUN., DUKE, MAJ. and COL.
List, Reginald, while I confess	My jealousy I can't express,
A love that's all unselfishness;	Their love they openly confess;
That it's unselfish, goodness knows,	His shell-like ears he does not close
You won't dispute it, I suppose?	To their recital of their woes.

DRAGOONS.

Oh, list while they a love confess
　　That words imperfectly express.
His shell-like ears, ah, do not close.
　　To blighted love's distracting woes!
　　　Now is not this ridiculous, etc.

END OF ACT I

Act II

Scene.—*A glade.* Jane *is discovered leaning on a violoncello, upon which she presently accompanies herself. Chorus of Maidens are heard singing in the distance.*

On such eyes as maidens cherish
　　Let thy fond adorers gaze,
　　Or incontinently perish,
In their all-consuming rays!

Jane: The fickle crew have deserted Reginald and sworn allegiance to his rival, and all, forsooth, because he has glanced with passing favour on a puling milkmaid! Fools! Of that fancy he will soon weary—and then, I, who alone am faithful to him, shall reap my reward. But do not dally too long, Reginald, for my charms are ripe, Reginald, and already they are decaying. Better secure me ere I have gone too far!

Recitative—Jane.

Sad is that woman's lot who, year by year,
Sees, one by one, her beauties disappear,
When Time, grown weary of her heart-drawn sighs,
Impatiently begins to "dim her eyes!"
Compelled, at last, in life's uncertain gloamings,
To wreathe her wrinkled brow with well-saved "combings",
Reduced, with rouge, lip-salve, and pearly grey,
To "make up" for lost time as best she may!

Song—Jane.

Silvered is the raven hair,
　　Spreading is the parting straight,
Mottled the complexion fair,
　　Halting is the youthful gait,
Hollow is the laughter free,
　　Spectacled the limpid eye,
Little will be left of me
　　In the coming bye and bye!

Fading is the taper waist,
    Shapeless grows the shapely limb,
And although severely laced,
    Spreading is the figure trim!
Stouter than I used to be,
    Still more corpulent grow I—
There will be too much of me
    In the coming by-and-bye!

(*Exit* JANE)

(*Enter* GROSVENOR, *followed by* MAIDENS, *two and two, each playing on an archaic instrument, as in Act I. He is reading abstractedly, as* BUNTHORNE *did in Act I, and pays no attention to them*)

CHORUS OF MAIDENS.

Turn, oh, turn in this direction,
    Shed, oh, shed a gentle smile,
With a glance of sad perfection,
    Our poor fainting hearts beguile!
On such eyes as maidens cherish
    Let thy fond adorers gaze,
Or incontinently perish,
    In their all-consuming rays!

(*He sits, they group around him*)

GROS.: (*aside*) The old, old tale. How rapturously these maidens love me, and how hopelessly! Oh, Patience, Patience, with the love of thee in my heart, what have I for these poor mad maidens but an unvalued pity? Alas, they will die of hopeless love for me, as I shall die of hopeless love for thee!

ANGELA: Sir, will it please you read to us?

GROS.: (*sighing*) Yes, child, if you will. What shall I read?

ANGELA: One of your own poems.

GROS.: One of my own poems? Better not, my child. *They* will not cure thee of thy love.

ELLA: Mr. Bunthorne used to read us a poem of his own every day.

SAPHIR: And, to do him justice, he read them extremely well.

GROS.: Oh, did he so? Well, who am I that I should take upon myself to withhold my gifts from you? What am I but a trustee? Here is a decalet—a pure and simple thing, a very daisy—a babe might understand it. To appreciate it, it is not necessary to think of anything at all.

ANGELA: Let us think of nothing at all!

GROS.: (*recites*)

> Gentle Jane was as good as gold,
> She always did as she was told;
> She never spoke when her mouth was full,
>> Or caught bluebottles their legs to pull,
>> Or spilt plum jam on her nice new frock,
>> Or put white mice in the eight-day clock,
>> Or vivisected her last new doll,
>> Or fostered a passion for alcohol.
> And when she grew up she was given in marriage
> To a first-class earl who keeps his carriage!

GROS.: I believe I am right in saying that there is not one word in that decalet which is calculated to bring the blush of shame to the cheek of modesty.

ANGELA: Not one; it is purity itself.

GROS.: Here's another.

> Teasing Tom was a very bad boy,
> A great big squirt was his favourite toy;
> He put live shrimps in his father's boots,
> And sewed up the sleeves of his Sunday suits;
> He punched his poor little sisters' heads,
> And cayenne-peppered their four-post beds;
> He plastered their hair with cobbler's wax,
> And dropped hot halfpennies down their backs.
> The consequence was he was lost tot*ally*,
> And married a girl in the *corps de bally*!

ANGELA: Marked you how grandly—how relentlessly—the damning catalogue of crime strode on, till Retribution, like a poisèd hawk, came swooping down upon the Wrong-Doer? Oh, it was terrible!

ELLA: Oh, sir, you are indeed a true poet, for you touch our hearts, and they go out to you!

GROS.: (*aside*) This is simply cloying. (*Aloud*) Ladies, I am sorry to appear ungallant, but this is Saturday, and you have been following me about ever since Monday. I should like the usual half-holiday. I shall take it as a personal favour if you will kindly allow me to close early to-day.

SAPHIR: Oh, sir, do not send us from you!

GROS.: Poor, poor girls! It is best to speak plainly. I know that I am loved by you, but I never can love you in return, for my heart is fixed elsewhere! Remember the fable of the Magnet and the Churn.

ANGELA: (*wildly*) But we don't know the fable of the Magnet and the Churn!

GROS.: Don't you? Then I will sing it to you.

SONG—GROSVENOR.

A magnet hung in a hardware shop,
And all around was a loving crop
Of scissors and needles, nails and knives,
Offering love for all their lives;
But for iron the magnet felt no whim,
Though he charmed iron, it charmed not him;
From needles and nails and knives he'd turn,
For he'd set his love on a Silver Churn!

MAIDENS: A Silver Churn?

GROSVENOR: A Silver Churn!
His most æsthetic,
Very magnetic
Fancy took this turn—
"If I can wheedle
A knife or a needle,
Why not a Silver Churn?"

MAIDENS: His most æsthetic, etc.

GROSVENOR: And Iron and Steel expressed surprise,
The needles opened their well-drilled eyes,
The penknives felt "shut up", no doubt,
The scissors declared themselves "cut out",
The kettles they boiled with rage, 'tis said,
While every nail went off its head,
And hither and thither began to roam,
Till a hammer came up and drove them home.

MAIDENS: It drove them home?

GROSVENOR: It drove them home!
While this magnetic,
Peripatetic

Lover he lived to learn,
    By no endeavour
    Can magnet ever
Attract a Silver Churn!

MAIDENS: While this magnetic, etc.

(*They go off in low spirits, gazing back at him from time to time*)

GROS.: At last they are gone! What is this mysterious fascination that I seem to exercise over all I come across? A curse on my fatal beauty, for I am sick of conquests!

(PATIENCE *appears*)

PATIENCE: Archibald!

GROS.: (*Turns and sees her*) Patience!

PATIENCE: I have escaped with difficulty from my Reginald. I wanted to see you so much that I might ask you if you still love me as fondly as ever?

GROS.: Love you? If the devotion of a lifetime—(*Seizes her hand*)

PATIENCE: (*indignantly*) Hold! Unhand me, or I scream! (*He releases her*) If you are a gentleman, pray remember that I am another's! (*Very tenderly*) But you *do* love me, don't you?

GROS.: Madly, hopelessly, despairingly!

PATIENCE: That's right! I never can be yours; but that's right!

GROS.: And you love this Bunthorne?

PATIENCE: With a heart-whole ecstasy that withers, and scorches, and burns, and stings! (*Sadly*) It is my duty.

GROS.: Admirable girl! But you are not happy with him?

PATIENCE: Happy? I am miserable beyond description!

GROS.: That's right! I never can be yours; but that's right!

PATIENCE: But go now. I see dear Reginald approaching. Farewell, dear Archibald; I cannot tell you how happy it has made me to know that you still love me.

GROS.: Ah, if I only dared—(*Advances towards her*)

PATIENCE: Sir! this language to one who is promised to another! (*Tenderly*) Oh, Archibald, think of me sometimes, for my heart is breaking! He is unkind to me, and you would be so loving!

GROS.: Loving! (*Advances towards her*)

PATIENCE: Advance one step, and as I am a good and pure woman, I scream! (*Tenderly*) Farewell, Archibald! (*Sternly*) Stop there! (*Tenderly*) Think of me sometimes! (*Angrily*) Advance at your peril! Once more, adieu!

(GROSVENOR *sighs, gazes sorrowfully at her, sighs deeply, and exits. She bursts into tears*)
(*Enter* BUNTHORNE, *followed by* JANE. *He is moody and preoccupied*)

JANE *sings.*

In a doleful train
One and one I walk all day;
For I love in vain—
None so sorrowful as they
Who can only sigh and say,
Woe is me, alackaday!

BUN.: (*seeing* PATIENCE) Crying, eh? What are you crying about?

PATIENCE: I've only been thinking how dearly I love you!

BUN.: Love me! Bah!

JANE: Love him! Bah!

BUN.: (*to* JANE) Don't you interfere.

JANE: He always crushes me!

PATIENCE: (*going to him*) What is the matter, dear Reginald? If you have any sorrow, tell it to me, that I may share it with you. (*Sighing*) It is my duty!

BUN.: (*snappishly*) Whom were you talking with just now?

PATIENCE: With dear Archibald.

BUN.: (*furiously*) With dear Archibald! Upon my honour, this is too much!

JANE: A great deal too much!

BUN.: (*angrily to* JANE) Do be quiet!

JANE: Crushed again!

PATIENCE: I think he is the noblest, purest, and most perfect being I have ever met. But I don't love *him*. It is true that he is devotedly attached to me, but I don't love him. Whenever he grows affectionate, I scream. It is my duty! (*Sighing*)

BUN.: I dare say!

JANE: So do I! *I* dare say!

PATIENCE: Why, how could I love him and love you too? You can't love two people at once!

BUN.: Oh, can't you, though!

PATIENCE: No, you can't; I only wish you could.

BUN.: I don't believe you know what love is!

PATIENCE: (*sighing*) Yes, I do. There was a happy time when I didn't, but a bitter experience has taught me.
(*Exeunt* BUNTHORNE *and* JANE)

BALLAD—PATIENCE.

Love is a plaintive song,
 Sung by a suffering maid,
Telling a tale of wrong,
 Telling of hope betrayed;
Tuned to each changing note,
 Sorry when *he* is sad,
Blind to his ev'ry mote,
 Merry when he is glad!
  Love that no wrong can cure,
   Love that is always new,
  That is the love that's pure,
   That is the love that's true!

Rendering good for ill,
 Smiling at every frown,
Yielding your own self-will,
 Laughing your tear-drops down;
Never a selfish whim,
 Trouble, or pain to stir;
Everything for him,
 Nothing at all for her!
  Love that will aye endure,
   Though the rewards be few,
  That is the love that's pure,
   That is the love that's true!

(*At the end of ballad exit* PATIENCE, *weeping. Enter* BUNTHORNE, *and* JANE)
BUN.: Everything has gone wrong with me since that smug-faced idiot came here. Before that I was admired—I may say, loved.
JANE: Too mild—adored!
BUN.: Do let a poet soliloquize! The damozels used to follow me wherever I went; now they all follow him!
JANE: Not all! *I* am still faithful to you.
BUN.: Yes, and a pretty damozel *you* are!

JANE: No, not pretty. Massive. Cheer up! I will never leave you, I swear it!

BUN.: Oh, thank you! I know what it is; it's his confounded mildness. They find me too highly spiced, if you please! And no doubt I *am* highly spiced.

JANE: Not for my taste!

BUN.: (*savagely*) No, but I am for theirs. But I will show the world I can be as mild as he. If they want insipidity, they shall have it. I'll meet this fellow on his own ground and beat him on it.

JANE: You shall. And I will help you.

BUN.: You will? Jane, there's a good deal of good in you, after all!

DUET—BUNTHORNE *and* JANE.

JANE: So go to him and say to him, with compliment ironical—

BUNTHORNE: Sing "Hey to you—
     Good-day to you"—
     And that's what I shall say!

JANE: "Your style is much too sanctified—your cut is too canonical"—

BUNTHORNE: Sing "Bah to you—
     Ha! ha! to you"—
   And that's what I shall say!

JANE: "I was the beau ideal of the morbid young æsthetical—
     To doubt my inspiration was regarded as heretical—
     Until you cut me out with your placidity emetical."

BUNTHORNE: Sing "Booh to you—
     Pooh, pooh to you"—
   And that's what I shall say!
     Sing "Booh to you—
     Pooh, pooh to you"—
   And that's what I shall say!

BOTH: Sing "Hey to you—good-day to you"—
     Sing "Bah to you—ha! ha! to you"—
     Sing "Booh to you—pooh, pooh to you"—
   And that's what you should/I shall say!

BUNTHORNE: I'll tell him that unless he will consent to be more jocular—

JANE: Sing "Booh to you—
     Pooh, pooh to you"—
   And that's what you should say!

BUNTHORNE: To cut his curly hair, and stick an eyeglass in his ocular—
JANE: Sing "Bah to you—
     Ha! ha! to you—"
And that's what you should say!
BUNTHORNE: To stuff his conversation full of quibble and of quiddity,
     To dine on chops and roly-poly pudding with avidity—
     He'd better clear away with all convenient rapidity.
JANE: Sing "Hey to you—
     Good-day to you"—
And that's what you should say!
BUNTHORNE: Sing "Booh to you—
     Pooh, pooh to you"—
And that's what you should say!
BOTH: Sing "Hey to you—good-day to you"—
     Sing "Bah to you—ha! ha! to you"—
     Sing "Booh to you—pooh, pooh to you"—
     And that's what you should/I shall say!

(*Exeunt* JANE *and* BUNTHORNE *together*)

(*Enter* DUKE, COLONEL, *and* MAJOR. *They have abandoned their uniforms, and are dressed and made up in imitation of Æsthetics. They have long hair, and other signs of attachment to the brotherhood. As they sing they walk in stiff, constrained, and angular attitudes—a grotesque exaggeration of the attitudes adopted by* BUNTHORNE *and the* MAIDENS *in Act I*)

TRIO—DUKE, COLONEL, *and* MAJOR.

It's clear that medieval art alone retains its zest,
To charm and please its devotees we've done our little best.
We're not quite sure if all we do has the Early English ring;
But, as far as we can judge, it's something like this sort of thing:
     You hold yourself like this, (*attitude*)
     You hold yourself like that, (*attitude*)
By hook and crook you try to look both angular and flat (*attitude*)
     We venture to expect
     That what we recollect,
Though but a part of true High Art, will have its due effect.

If this is not exactly right, we hope you won't upbraid;
You can't get high Æsthetic tastes, like trousers, ready made.

True views on Mediævalism Time alone will bring,
But, as far as we can judge, it's something like this sort of thing:
    You hold yourself like this, (*attitude*)
    You hold yourself like that, (*attitude*)
By hook and crook you try to look both angular and flat (*attitude*)
    To cultivate the trim
    Rigidity of limb,
You ought to get a Marionette, and form your style on him
    (*attitude*)

COLONEL: (*attitude*) Yes, it's quite clear that our only chance of making a lasting impression on these young ladies is to become as æsthetic as they are.

MAJOR: (*attitude*) No doubt. The only question is how far we've succeeded in doing so. I don't know why, but I've an idea that this is not quite right.

DUKE: (*attitude*) *I* don't like it. I never did. I don't see what it means. I do it, but I don't like it.

COLONEL: My good friend, the question is not whether we like it, but whether they do. They understand these things—we don't. Now I shouldn't be surprised if this is effective enough—at a distance.

MAJOR: I can't help thinking we're a little stiff at it. It would be extremely awkward if we were to be "struck" so!

COLONEL: I don't think we shall be struck so. Perhaps we're a little awkward at first—but everything must have a beginning. Oh, here they come! 'Tention!

(*They strike fresh attitudes, as* ANGELA *and* SAPHIR *enter*)

ANGELA: (*seeing them*) Oh, Saphir—see—see! The immortal fire has descended on them, and they are of the Inner Brotherhood— perceptively intense and consummately utter.

(*The* OFFICERS *have some difficulty in maintaining their constrained attitudes*)

SAPHIR: (*in admiration*) How Botticelian! How Fra Angelican! Oh, Art, we thank thee for this boon!

COLONEL: (*apologetically*) I'm afraid we're not quite right.

ANGELA: Not supremely, perhaps, but oh, so all-but! (*To* SAPHIR) Oh, Saphir, are they not quite too all-but?

SAPHIR: They are indeed jolly utter!

MAJOR: (*in agony*) I wonder what the Inner Brotherhood usually recommend for cramp?

COLONEL: Ladies, we will not deceive you. We are doing this at some personal inconvenience with a view of expressing the extremity of our devotion to you. We trust that it is not without its effect.

ANGELA: We will not deny that we are much moved by this proof of your attachment.

SAPHIR: Yes, your conversion to the principles of Æsthetic Art in its highest development has touched us deeply.

ANGELA: And if Mr. Grosvenor should remain obdurate—

SAPHIR: Which we have every reason to believe he will—

MAJOR: (*aside, in agony*) I wish they'd make haste!

ANGELA: We are not prepared to say that our yearning hearts will not go out to you.

COLONEL: (*as giving a word of command*) By sections of threes— Rapture! (*All strike a fresh attitude, expressive of æsthetic rapture*)

SAPHIR: Oh, it's extremely good—for beginners it's admirable.

MAJOR: The only question is, who will take who?

COLONEL: Oh, the Duke chooses first, as a matter of course.

DUKE: Oh, I couldn't thank of it—you are really too good!

COLONEL: Nothing of the kind. You are a great matrimonial fish, and it's only fair that each of these ladies should have a chance of hooking you.[1]

---

1. In early performances, the dialogue continued:

> DUKE: Won't that be rather awkward
> COLONEL: Awkward, not at all. Observe, suppose you choose Angela, I take Saphir, Major takes nobody. Suppose you choose Saphir, Major takes Angela, I take nobody. Suppose you choose neither, I take Angela, Major takes Saphir. Clear as day!
> ANGELA: Capital!
> SAPHIR: The very thing!

In *Original Plays, Third Series,* this is shortened to:

> DUKE: It's perfectly simple. Observe, suppose you choose Angela, I take Saphir, Major takes nobody. Suppose you choose Saphir, Major takes Angela, I take nobody. Suppose you choose neither, I take Angela, Major takes Saphir. Clear as day!

Some libretti give the Duke's speech to the Colonel.

QUINTET.

DUKE: (*Taking* SAPHIR)
    If Saphir I choose to marry,
        I shall be fixed up for life;
    Then the Colonel need not tarry,
        Angela can be his wife.
(*Handing* ANGELA *to* COLONEL)
(DUKE *dances with* SAPHIR, COLONEL *with* ANGELA, MAJOR *dances alone*)
MAJOR: In that case unprecedented,
        Single I shall live and die—
    I shall have to be contented
        With their heartfelt sympathy!
ALL: (*dancing as before*) He will have to be contented
        With our heartfelt sympathy!
    In that case unprecedented, etc.
DUKE: (*Taking* ANGELA)
    If on Angy I determine,
        At my wedding she'll appear,
    Decked in diamond and ermine.
        Major then can take Saphir!
(*Handing* SAPHIR *to* MAJOR)
(DUKE *dances with* ANGELA, MAJOR *with* SAPHIR, COLONEL *dances alone*)
COLONEL: (*dancing*)
    In that case unprecedented,
        Single I shall live and die—
    I shall have to be contented
        With their heartfelt sympathy!
ALL: (*dancing as before*)
    He will have to be contented
        With our heartfelt sympathy! (etc.)
DUKE: (*Taking both* ANGELA *and* SAPHIR)
    After some debate internal,
        If on neither I decide,
    Saphir then can take the Colonel,
(*Handing* SAPHIR *to* COLONEL)
    Angy be the Major's bride!
(*Handing* ANGELA *to* MAJOR)

DUKE: (*dancing*) In that case unprecedented,
    Single I shall live and die—
I shall have to be contented
    With their heartfelt sympathy!
ALL: (*dancing as before*)
    He will have to be contented
      With our heartfelt sympathy! (etc.)

(*At the end,* DUKE, COLONEL, *and* MAJOR, *and two girls dance off arm-in-arm*)

(*Enter* GROSVENOR)

GROS.: It is very pleasant to be alone. It is pleasant to be able to gaze at leisure upon those features which all others may gaze upon at their good will! (*Looking at his reflection in hand-mirror*) Ah, I am a very Narcissus!

(*Enter* BUNTHORNE, *moodily*)

BUN.: It's no use; I can't live without admiration. Since Grosvenor came here, insipidity has been at a premium. Ah, he is there!

GROS.: Ah, Bunthorne! Come here—look! Very graceful, isn't it!

BUN.: (*taking hand-mirror*) Allow me; I haven't seen it. Yes, it is graceful.

GROS.: (*taking back the mirror*) Oh, good gracious! not that—this—

BUN.: You don't mean that! Bah! I am in no mood for trifling.

GROS.: And what is amiss?

BUN.: Ever since you came here, you have entirely monopolized the attentions of the young ladies. I don't like it, sir!

GROS.: My dear sir, how can I help it? They are the plague of my life. My dear Mr. Bunthorne, with your personal disadvantages, you can have no idea of the inconvenience of being madly loved, at first sight, by every woman you meet.

BUN.: Sir, until you came here I was adored!

GROS.: Exactly—until I came here. That's my grievance. I cut everybody out! I assure you, if you could only suggest some means whereby, consistently with my duty to society, I could escape these inconvenient attentions, you would earn my everlasting gratitude.

BUN.: I will do so at once. However popular it may be with the world at large, your personal appearance is highly objectionable to *me*.

GROS.: It is? (*Shaking his hand*) Oh, thank you! thank you! How can I express my gratitude?

BUN.: By making a complete change at once. Your conversation must henceforth be perfectly matter-of-fact. You must cut your hair, and have a back parting. In appearance and costume you must be absolutely commonplace.

GROS.: (*decidedly*) No. Pardon me, that's impossible.

BUN.: Take care! When I am thwarted I am very terrible.

GROS.: I can't help that. I am a man with a mission. And that mission must be fulfilled.

BUN.: I don't think you quite appreciate the consequences of thwarting me.

GROS.: I don't care what they are.

BUN.: Suppose—I won't go so far as to say that I will do it—but suppose for one moment I were to curse you? (GROSVENOR *quails*) Ah! Very well. Take care.

GROS.: But surely you would never do that? (*In great alarm*)

BUN.: I don't know. It would be an extreme measure, no doubt. Still—

GROS.: (*wildly*) But you would not do it—I am sure you would not. (*Throwing himself at* BUNTHORNE's *knees, and clinging to him*) Oh, reflect, reflect! You had a mother once.

BUN.: Never!

GROS.: Then you had an aunt! (BUNTHORNE *affected*) Ah! I see you had! By the memory of that aunt, I implore you to pause ere you resort to this last fearful expedient. Oh, Mr. Bunthorne, reflect, reflect! (*Weeping*)

BUN.: (*aside, after a struggle with himself*) I must not allow myself to be unmanned! (*Aloud*) It is useless. Consent at once, or may a nephew's curse—

GROS.: Hold! Are you absolutely resolved?

BUN.: Absolutely.

GROS.: Will nothing shake you?

BUN.: Nothing. I am adamant.

GROS.: Very good. (*Rising*) Then I yield.

BUN.: Ha! You swear it?

GROS.: I do, cheerfully. I have long wished for a reasonable pretext for such a change as you suggest. It has come at last. I do it on compulsion!

BUN.: Victory! I triumph!

DUET—BUNTHORNE *and* GROSVENOR.

BUNTHORNE: When I go out of door,
　　　Of damozels a score

      (All sighing and burning,
      And clinging and yearning)
  Will follow me as before.
  I shall, with cultured taste,
  Distinguish gems from paste,
      And "High diddle diddle"
      Will rank as an idyll,
  If I pronounce it chaste!
BOTH: A most intense young man,
      A soulful-eyed young man,
  An ultra-poetical, super-æsthetical,
      Out-of-the-way young man!
GROSVENOR: Conceive me, if you can,
  An every-day young man:
      A commonplace type,
      With a stick and a pipe,
  And a half-bred black-and-tan;
      Who thinks suburban "hops"
      More fun than "Monday Pops",
  Who's fond of his dinner,
  And doesn't get thinner
      On bottled beer and chops.
BOTH: A commonplace young man,
      A matter-of-fact young man,
  A steady and stolid-y, jolly Bank-holiday,
      Every-day young man!
BUNTHORNE: A Japanese young man,
      A blue-and-white young man,
  Francesca di Rimini, miminy, pimini,
      Je-ne-sais-quoi young man!
GROSVENOR: A Chancery lane young man,
      A Somerset House young man,
  A very delectable, highly respectable
      Threepenny-bus young man!
BUNTHORNE: A pallid and thin young man,
      A haggard and lank young man,
  A greenery-yallery, Grosvenor Gallery,
      Foot-in-the-grave young man!
GROSVENOR: A Sewell & Cross young man,

A Howell & James young man,
A pushing young particle—"What's the next article?"—
Waterloo House young man!

BUNTHORNE.	GROSVENOR.
Conceive me, if you can,	Conceive me, if you can,
A crotchety, cracked young man,	A matter-of-fact young man,
An ultra-poetical, super-æsthetical,	An alphabetical, arithmetical,
Out-of-the way young man!	Everyday young man!

(*At the end,* GROSVENOR *dances off.* BUNTHORNE *remains*)

BUN.: It is all right! I have committed my last act of ill-nature, and henceforth I'm a changed character.

(*Dances about stage, humming refrain of last air. Enter* PATIENCE. *She gazes in astonishment at him*)

PATIENCE: Reginald! Dancing! And—what in the world is the matter with you?

BUN.: Patience, I'm a changed man. Hitherto I've been gloomy, moody, fitful—uncertain in temper and selfish in disposition—

PATIENCE: You have, indeed! (*Sighing*)

BUN.: All that is changed. I have reformed. I have modelled myself upon Mr. Grosvenor. Henceforth I am mildly cheerful. My conversation will blend amusement with instruction. I shall still be æsthetic; but my æstheticism will be of the most pastoral kind.

PATIENCE: Oh, Reginald! Is all this true?

BUN.: Quite true. Observe how amiable I am. (*Assuming a fixed smile*)

PATIENCE: But, Reginald, how long will this last?

BUN.: With occasional intervals for rest and refreshment, as long as I do.

PATIENCE: Oh, Reginald, I'm so happy! (*In his arms*) Oh, dear, dear Reginald, I cannot express the joy I feel at this change. It will no longer be a duty to love you, but a pleasure—a rapture—an ecstasy!

BUN.: My darling!

PATIENCE: But—oh, horror! (*Recoiling from him*)

BUN.: What's the matter?

PATIENCE: Is it quite certain that you have absolutely reformed—that you are henceforth a perfect being—utterly free from defect of any kind?

BUN.: It is quite certain. I have sworn it.

PATIENCE: Then I never can be yours!

BUN.: Why not?

PATIENCE: Love, to be pure, must be absolutely unselfish, and there can be nothing unselfish in loving so perfect a being as you have now become!

BUN.: But, stop a bit. I don't want to change—I'll relapse—I'll be as I was—interrupted!

(*Enter* GROSVENOR, *followed by all the 'every-day young girls', who are followed by* CHORUS OF DRAGOONS. *He has had his hair cut, and is dressed in an ordinary suit of dittoes and a pot hat. They all dance cheerfully round the stage in marked contrast to their former languor*)

CHORUS—GROSVENOR *and* GIRLS.

GROSVENOR: I'm a Waterloo House young man,
 A Sewell & Cross young man,
A steady and stolid-y, jolly Bank-holiday,
 Every-day young man.

GIRLS: We're Swears & Wells young girls,
 We're Madame Louise young girls,
We're prettily pattering, cheerily chattering,
 Every-day young girls.

BUN.: Angela—Ella—Saphir—what—what does this mean?

ANGELA: It means that Archibald the All-Right cannot be all-wrong; and if the All-Right chooses to discard æstheticism, it proves that æstheticism ought to be discarded.

PATIENCE: Oh, Archibald! Archibald! I'm shocked—surprised—horrified!

GROS.: I can't help it. I'm not a free agent. I do it on compulsion.

PATIENCE: This is terrible. Go! I shall never set eyes on you again. But—oh, joy!

GROS.: What is the matter?

PATIENCE: Is it quite, quite certain that you will always be a commonplace young man?

GROS.: Always—I've sworn it.

PATIENCE: Why, then, there's nothing to prevent my loving you with all the fervour at my command!

GROS.: Why, that's true.

PATIENCE: My Archibald!

GROS.: My Patience! (*They embrace*)

BUN.: Crushed again!

(*Enter* JANE)

JANE: (*who is still æsthetic*) Cheer up! I am still here. I have never left you, and I never will!

BUN.: Thank you, Jane. After all, there is no denying it, you're a fine figure of a woman!

JANE: My Reginald!

BUN.: My Jane!

(*Flourish. Enter* COLONEL, MAJOR, *and* DUKE)

COLONEL: Ladies, the Duke has at length determined to select a bride! (*General excitement*)

DUKE: I have a great gift to bestow. Approach, such of you as are truly lovely. (*All come forward, bashfully, except* JANE *and* PATIENCE) In personal appearance you have all that is necessary to make a woman happy. In common fairness, I think I ought to choose the only one among you who has the misfortune to be distinctly plain. (*Girls retire disappointed*) Jane!

JANE: (*leaving* BUNTHORNE's *arms*) Duke! (JANE *and* DUKE *embrace.* BUNTHORNE *is utterly disgusted*)

BUN.: Crushed again!

FINALE.

DUKE: After much debate internal,
    I on Lady Jane decide,
  Saphir now may take the Colonel,
    Angy be the Major's bride!

(SAPHIR *pairs off with* COLONEL, ANGELA *with* MAJOR, ELLA *with* SOLICITOR)

BUNTHORNE: In that case unprecedented,
    Single I must live and die—
  I shall have to be contented
    With a tulip or li*l*y!

(*Takes a lily from button-hole and gazes affectionately at it*)

ALL: He will have to be contented
    With a tulip or li*l*y!
  In that case unprecedented (etc.)

Greatly pleased with one another,
    To get married we/they decide.
Each of us/them will wed the other,
    Nobody be Bunthorne's Bride!

DANCE

END OF OPERA

A Note About the Author

W.S. Gilbert (1836–1911) and Arthur Sullivan (1842–1900) were theatrical collaborators during the nineteenth century. Prior to their partnership, Gilbert wrote and illustrated stories as a child, eventually developing his signature "topsy-turvy" style. Sullivan was raised in a musical family where he learned to play multiple instruments at an early age. Together, their talents would help produce a successful series of comic operas. Some notable titles include *The Pirates of Penzance*, *The Sorcerer*, *H.M.S. Pinafore*, and *The Mikado*.

A Note from the Publisher

Spanning many genres, from non-fiction essays to literature classics to children's books and lyric poetry, Mint Edition books showcase the master works of our time in a modern new package. The text is freshly typeset, is clean and easy to read, and features a new note about the author in each volume. Many books also include exclusive new introductory material. Every book boasts a striking new cover, which makes it as appropriate for collecting as it is for gift giving. Mint Edition books are only printed when a reader orders them, so natural resources are not wasted. We're proud that our books are never manufactured in excess and exist only in the exact quantity they need to be read and enjoyed.

bookfinity™

Discover more of your favorite classics with Bookfinity™.

- Track your reading with custom book lists.
- Get great book recommendations for your personalized Reader Type.
- Add reviews for your favorite books.
- AND MUCH MORE!

Visit **bookfinity.com** and take the fun Reader Type quiz to get started.

Enjoy our classic and modern companion pairings!

Classic & Modern

www.ingramcontent.com/pod-product-compliance
Lightning Source LLC
Chambersburg PA
CBHW020608030426
42337CB00013B/1276